HOW TO COOK
FRENCH
CUISINE

50 traditional French recipes

Laurent Valentinuz would like to thank
Bruno Leprieur and Gezebel Domet

© Tana éditions, a department of Édi8, 2016

ISBN: 979-10-301-0096-9
Legal deposit: January 2016
Printed in Slovenia

Tana éditions, a department of Édi8
12, avenue d'Italie
75013 Paris
Tel.: 01 44 16 09 00
Fax: 01 44 16 09 01
www.tana.fr

Director of publication: Laurent Valentinuz
Graphic design: Stéphanie Boulay
Translation: Ruth Clarke
Layout and editorial assistance: Sophie Greloux

JULIE SOUCAIL

HOW TO COOK
FRENCH
CUISINE

50 traditional French recipes

PHOTOGRAPHER
FABRICE VEIGAS

Tana
éditions

CONTENTS

Desserts **75**

Index **106**

Starters

ASPARAGUS

mousseline sauce

- 2 bunches of asparagus
- 1 pinch coarse salt
- 1 tsp. Maïzena®/corn starch
- 70 g/⅝ cup double cream, well chilled
- 2 egg yolks
- 130 g/⅝ cup butter
- 1 dash lemon juice
- 2 sprigs parsley, leaves only, chopped

Salt

Remove the tough ends of the asparagus spears, wash and tie in a bunch.

Pour water into a tall saucepan and heat until simmering. Add the salt and place the asparagus into the pan, tips upwards (the tips must not be submerged), cook for 10 to 12 minutes. Check that they are fully cooked by inserting the blade of a knife into the base of one of the spears.

Meanwhile, prepare the mousseline sauce: dilute the Maïzena® in a little water. Whip the cream. Prepare a bain-marie and add the egg yolks, salt and 1 tbsp. cold water. Stir until the mixture is even.

Remove from heat, stir in the corn starch mixture and then the butter, cut into blocks. Let the sauce thicken over a low heat in the bain-marie. When the sauce is thick and smooth, stir in the whipped cream and lemon juice.

Serve the asparagus warm, topped with mousseline sauce and sprinkled with finely chopped parsley.

This delicate sauce brings out the flavour of the asparagus and adds a real touch of Spring to your plate.

HERRING

AND *potato salad*

- 1 egg
- 2 medium sized firm potatoes
- 1½ herring fillets
- ¼ red onion
- 1½ tbsp. olive oil
- 1 sprig flat parsley
- Salt, freshly ground pepper

Hard boil an egg - cook for 10 minutes once it reaches boiling point.

Wash the potatoes and cook with the skins on until still slightly firm. Drain, leave to cool, then peel. Cut into thick slices.

Peel the egg and cut into quarters.

Chop the herring fillets into 2 cm pieces.

Peel and chop the red onion.

Place all the ingredients into a small bowl, sprinkle with olive oil, season with salt and pepper and mix.

Remove the parsley leaves, chop and sprinkle over the salad.

PÂTÉ EN CROÛTE

For the pastry
- 450 g/3⅔ cups flour
- 1 egg+1 for egg wash
- 2 tsp. salt
- 130 g/½ cup butter at room temperature
- 15 cl/⅝ cup of water

For the filling
- 1 small onion chopped
- 4 shallots chopped
- 250 g/9 oz. cured ham
- 400 g/14 oz. spare rib of pork
- 400 g/14 oz. neck or shoulder of veal
- 8 cl /⅓ cup port
- 1 tsp. salt
- 1 pinch nutmeg
- 1 pinch all spice
- 6 turns of freshly ground white pepper
- 1 sprig thyme
- 1 bay leaf
- 2 eggs beaten
- 1 handful shelled pistachios
- 1 sachet instant gelatine

Prepare the pastry: pour the flour into a bowl, make a well for the eggs and salt, add the butter cut into pieces. Mix, then knead, incorporating the water. When the dough is smooth, make a ball and leave to stand for 1 hour in the refrigerator.

Prepare the filling: cut the ham into cubes. Remove the fat from the other meat, cut half into cubes and mince the rest. Mix the meat in a bowl, add the port, onion, shallots, salt, nutmeg, allspice and white pepper. Stir, add the thyme and bay leaf, then cover and leave to marinate for 2 hours in the refrigerator.

Roll out the pastry 3 mm thick, cut one rectangle to cover the bottom and sides across the width of the tin. Then cut two small rectangles and place them on the empty sides. Press well to seal the pastry strips together. Roll out the remaining dough and cut out a last rectangle to cover. Preheat the oven to 410°F.

Take the filling from the refrigerator, remove the thyme and bay leaf, add the eggs and crushed pistachios, mix again. Place the filling in the tin. Place the last rectangle of pastry over the filling and press the edges together firmly.

Beat an egg with 2 tsp. water and glaze the pastry. Make two holes in the top of the pastry, slide in 2 pieces of baking paper rolled into tubes. Bake for 1 hour. Remove the pie from the dish while still warm, then leave to cool on a rack.

Prepare the gelatine according to the instructions on the packet. Place the pie on a sheet of baking paper and pour the gelatine into the holes. Repeat this several times to let the gelatine spread. Chill for 12 hours.

LEEKS
WITH
vinaigrette

- 2 eggs
- 8 medium leeks
- 1 tsp. mustard
- 3 tbsp. lemon juice
- 6 tbsp. neutral oil
- 5 bunches parsley
- Salt, pepper

Hard boil the eggs. Start cooking in cold water and continue for 10 minutes once the water begins to boil. Rinse under cold water.

Steam the leeks for 10-15 minutes depending on their size, use the blade of a knife to check that they are properly cooked, they should be nice and soft.

Remove the egg shells, finely chop the whites and set the yolks aside.

Emulsify the mustard, lemon juice and 1 pinch of salt, add the oil, whisking. Season with pepper.

Remove the parsley leaves and chop.

Place the leeks in a large bowl, drizzle with the vinaigrette and sprinkle with chopped egg white. Crush the yolks over the plate, using a fine strainer. Finish with finely chopped parsley.

This light and simple recipe requires perfectly cooked leeks – and that's the only hard part!

Serves **4** ∥ Preparation: **15** min ∥ Cooking: **5** min

PERIGOURD
salad

- 1 large romaine lettuce
- 5 sprigs parsley
- 4 tomatoes
- 1 small tin sweetcorn
- 1 tsp. strong mustard
- 2 tbsp. good quality wine vinegar
- 3 tbsp. nut oil
- 2 tbsp. sunflower oil
- 250 g/9 oz. gizzards
- 120 g/4.2 oz. dried duck breast
- 1 handful walnut kernels
- Salt, freshly ground pepper

Thoroughly wash and spin the salad and parsley. Chop the parsley. Wash the tomatoes and cut into quarters, drain the corn.

Emulsify the mustard and vinegar with a pinch of salt. Stir in the oil, whisking. Season with pepper.

Place the vegetables in a large bowl, add half the vinaigrette and mix well.

Heat a frying pan, wipe the gizzards to remove grease, slice into strips, heat through for a few minutes and keep warm.

Place the gizzards and slices of duck breast on top of the salad, drizzle with the remaining dressing and sprinkle with chopped parsley and walnuts.

FARMHOUSE
terrine

- 200 g/7 oz.pork belly
- 200 g/7 oz pork shoulder
- 150 g/5 oz. pork liver
- 1 onion
- 80 g/3 oz. bread
- 5 cl/⅕ cup milk
- 2 eggs
- 10 g/2 tsp. salt
- 2 g/½ tsp. black pepper
- 1 pinch Espelette pepper
- 100 g/3.5 oz. pork caul
- 1 bay leaf
- 1 sprig thyme

Cut the meat into pieces. Peel and coarsely chop the onion. Cut the bread into pieces and soak in milk. Mix all these ingredients in a bowl, then coarsely mince the mixture in a blender.

Mix the previous preparation with the eggs, salt, pepper and Espelette pepper in a bowl.

Preheat the oven to 350°F.

Rinse the caul with lukewarm water and drain. Pack it into the bottom of a pot, letting it hang over all sides and fill with the stuffing. Pack down well. Place the bay leaf and thyme on top and fold the caul around the whole thing. Cover with the lid.

Place the pot in a bain-marie and bake for 45 minutes. The terrine is cooked when the tip of a knife comes out clean and warm. Leave to cool then refrigerate for 48 hours.

FRENCH ONION

- 4 large onions
- 40 g/2 heaped tbsp. butter
- 10 g/1 level tbsp. flour
- 1 litre/4 cups water
- 25 cl/1 cup white wine
- 4 slices of bread
- 100 g/1 cup grated cheese
- Salt, pepper

Peel and thinly slice the onions. Heat the butter in a heavy bottomed pan and fry the onions for 15 minutes on a low heat, stirring regularly.

Sprinkle the onions with flour and stir for 3 minutes. Add the water and white wine and continue to stir, season with salt and pepper and cook for 15 minutes.

Pour the soup into 4 individual ovenproof bowls, add 1 slice of bread to each bowl and sprinkle with grated cheese.

Brown under the grill for about 5 minutes until the cheese is melted.

Serve hot.

Legend has it that the first onion soup was invented by Louis XV with onions, butter and champagne.

ROASTED
camembert

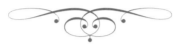

- 2 camembert cheeses,
  not too mature
- Salt, freshly ground pepper
- Accompaniments (optional)
- Chives
- Toast cut into fingers or cubes

Two possible cooking methods.
Oven.
Preheat the oven to 350°F. Open the boxes and remove the camembert cheeses from their packaging. Place them back into the boxes and close the lids. Bake for 20 minutes then remove the lids, place the cheeses under the grill and continue cooking for 15 minutes.

Open fire.
Open the boxes and remove the camembert cheeses from their packaging. Place them back into the boxes and wrap several times in aluminium foil. Place them in the embers of the fire and cook for around 15 minutes.

Using a knife, remove the cheese rind and season with salt and pepper. Serve hot, immediately, like a fondue in the middle of the table, with squares or fingers of toast and some chopped chives.

An easily prepared starter which puts this Normandy cheese, invented in the 19th century, in pride of place.

BAKED EGGS
SERVED WITH
foie gras

- 1 large slice of sliced bread
- 15 g/1 tbsp. butter
- 1 egg
- 2 tbsp. single cream
- 30 g/1 oz. semi-cooked foie gras
- Salt, freshly ground pepper

Cut the slice of bread into 4, lengthways.

Melt the butter in a pan and fry the bread until golden. Remove from the pan onto a paper towel.

Preheat the oven to 350°F.

Break the egg and separate the yolk from the white.
Mix the white with the single cream and season with salt and pepper.

Cut the foie gras into strips, removing the fat if necessary. Place the strips at the bottom of a ramekin, then add the cream.
Place the ramekin in a baking dish and add boiling water up to two thirds of the height of the ramekin.

Bake for 10 minutes, then add the egg yolk and cook for another 3 minutes.

Eat hot, served with buttered bread fingers and a green salad.

POACHED EGGS
in red wine sauce

- 1 cube chicken stock
- 15 cl/⅝ cup of water
- 180 g/6 oz. smoked lardons
- 1 large onion
- 1 tbsp. oil
- 20 g/2 level tbsp flour
- 70 cl/3 cups red wine
- 7 g/1 tsp. caster sugar
- 1 bouquet garni
- 50 g/¼ cup butter
- 6 slices crusty bread
- 10 cl/⅖ cup white vinegar
- 6 eggs
- 2 tbsp. chopped parsley
- Freshly ground pepper

Dissolve the chicken stock cube in hot water.

Brown the lardons in a large pan and set aside. Peel and thinly slice the onion. Pour the oil into a large saucepan and let the onion soften for a few minutes. Sprinkle with flour and cook for 2 to 3 minutes, stirring constantly. Pour the wine and stock into the saucepan, then add the sugar and bouquet garni. Mix well and allow to thicken over a low heat for 20 minutes, stirring occasionally. When the sauce is creamy, remove the bouquet garni and filter through a fine sieve. Add the butter cut into small pieces and the smoked lardons, season with pepper. Keep warm.

Toast the slices of crusty bread, arrange on plates.

Pour water into a saucepan, you'll need enough to cover the eggs. Add the vinegar and heat until the water is simmering. Break the first egg into a small cup and transfer it gently into the simmering water. Using a slotted spoon, fold the white around the yolk to give the egg a rounded shape. Cook for 4 minutes then remove the egg and drain on a paper towel. Repeat with the remaining eggs.

Place 1 egg in the middle of each slice of bread and pour the wine sauce over the top. Finish with a sprinkling of parsley.

A speciality from Burgundy. What are you waiting for? This recipe calls for a real Burgundy wine to bring out its finest flavours.

Mains

VEAL

stew

- 1 onion
- 3 cloves
- 600 g/21 oz. veal tendron
- 700 g/25 oz. veal shoulder
- 1 small carrot
- ½ bunch celery stalks
- 1 trimmed leek
- 1 bunch thyme
- 1 bay leaf
- 15 cl/⅝ cup dry white wine
- 15 small white onions
- 200 g/8 oz. mushrooms
- 1 lemon
- 40 g/2 heaped tbsp. butter
- 125 g/½ cup double cream
- 3 egg yolks
- 1 pinch freshly grated nutmeg
- Salt, freshly ground pepper

A staple of French cooking. Although you may not know that Blanquette can also be made using any white meat. Why not get creative?

Peel the onion and stud with cloves. Cut the meat into cubes. Peel the carrot. Wash the celery, carrot and leek. Place the meat in a casserole dish, add the vegetables, thyme, bay leaf, onion and wine, and cover with water. Season with salt and pepper. Bring to the boil for 5 minutes, removing any foam. Lower the heat and cook for 2 hours.

Top and tail the white onions, rinse and dry. Remove the earthy end of the mushrooms, wash and dry. Cut into quarters and drizzle with lemon juice.

Melt 20g/1½ tbsp. butter in a saucepan, add the onions and 5 cl/⅕ cup water, cook for 20 minutes until tender. Melt the remaining butter and sweat the mushrooms until all the liquid is absorbed. Stir the onions and mushrooms and keep warm. When the meat is cooked, remove from the casserole dish, add the onions and mushrooms, stir and keep warm.

Strain the cooking stock through a fine sieve. Place the stock over a high heat and reduce until there is 20 cl/⅞ cup left. Stir in the cream, bring to the boil for 1 minute and then turn off the heat. Take 1 ladle of stock and whisk it with the egg yolks.

Pour this mixture into the saucepan and thicken over a very low heat, whisking constantly for 15 seconds until the sauce is creamy. Add the nutmeg and the juice of ½ lemon and stir. Adjust seasoning if necessary. Pour the sauce over the meat, mix well and serve hot.

VEAL
paupiettes

- 180 g/6oz. mushrooms
- 125 g/5oz. ham
- 5 small shallots
- 125 g/4.5 oz. sausage meat
- 1 tbsp. chopped parsley
- 1 egg
- 6 wide, thin veal escalopes, 100 g/3.5 oz each
- 6 rashers bacon
- 2 tbsp. oil
- 100 g/3.5 oz. lardons
- 2 tbsp. flour
- 15 cl/⅝ cup white wine
- 40 g/1.5 oz. green olives
- 1 bouquet garni (thyme and bay leaf)
- Salt, freshly ground pepper

Chop 60 g/2 oz. mushrooms and the ham. Peel and chop 2 shallots. Mix everything together with the sausage meat, parsley and beaten egg.

Season one side of the escalopes with salt and pepper, spread the stuffing in the middle.

Fold the edges of the escalopes around the stuffing, roll the meatballs in a rasher of bacon and fasten tightly so that the stuffing does not escape during cooking.

Cut the remaining mushrooms into quarters. Peel and chop the remaining shallots.

Heat the oil in a casserole dish and brown the paupiettes. Remove them from the dish and replace with the shallots, mushrooms and bacon. Sauté for a few minutes then add the flour and stir for 2 minutes. Add the white wine, 10 cl/⅖ cup water, olives and bouquet garni. Simmer on a low heat for 40 minutes. Taste, season with pepper and add salt if necessary (the olives will already make the dish salty).

Serve hot.

BEEF
bourguignon

- 1 kg/35 oz. beef for braising
  (cheek, shin, shoulder, chuck)
- 1 onion
- 4 cloves
- 1 kg/35 oz. carrots
- 5 shallots
- 1 tsp. peppercorns
- 3 tbsp. oil
- 2 tbsp. flour
- 75 cl/1 bottle red wine
- 3 sprigs thyme
- 2 bay leaves
- 2 cubes beef stock
- 4 tbsp. chopped parsley
- Salt

Cut the meat into large cubes. Peel the onion and stud with cloves. Peel the carrots and shallots. Wash and dry the carrots and cut into slices. Finely chop the shallots. Lightly crush the peppercorns.

Heat the oil in a casserole dish and brown the meat on all sides. Remove it from the dish and replace with the chopped shallots. Soften over a low heat until translucent. Sprinkle with flour and cook for 2 to 3 minutes, stirring constantly. Add the red wine, thyme, bay leaf and peppercorns and crumble the stock cubes. Mix together, then add the meat, carrots and onion. Pour in enough water to cover the meat and cook, with a lid on, for 3 hours, stirring occasionally. 20 minutes before the end of cooking, remove the lid to let the sauce thicken. Taste and adjust seasoning if necessary.

Sprinkle with parsley and serve with steamed potatoes, tagliatelle or other fresh pasta.

Why bourguignon?
The dish owes its name to the two main ingredients, beef and wine, for which Burgundy is famous.

BEEF
tartare

- 1 tbsp. capers, preferably salted
- 3 shallots
- 600 g/21 oz. freshly ground
  prime quality beef
- 4 egg yolks
- 5 tbsp. strong mustard
- 3 tbsp. Worcestershire sauce
- 2 tbsp. olive oil
- 2 tbsp. chopped parsley
- 2 tbsp. de chopped chives
- A few drops of Tabasco®
- Salt, freshly ground
  pepper

If using salted capers, rinse under a running tap and leave to desalinate in a bowl of warm water for 1 hour, changing the water 2 or 3 times.

Peel and finely chop the shallots.

Drain and coarsely chop the capers.

Thoroughly mix the ground meat, egg yolks, mustard, Worcestershire sauce, olive oil, parsley, chives and chopped capers in a bowl. Add a few drops of Tabasco®, season with salt and pepper.

Compress one quarter of the mixture in a ramekin and turn out on a plate. Repeat this procedure with the rest of the mixture.

Enjoy immediately with homemade fries or a tangy green salad.

COTTAGE
pie

- 1 kg/35 oz. braising steak
- 3 onions
- 4 tbsp. olive oil
- 15 cl/⅝ cup red wine
- 1 cube beef stock
- 1 kg/35 oz. floury potatoes
- 6 shallots
- 125 g/½ cup butter
- 15 cl/⅝ cup milk
- 1.5 tbsp. thick double cream
- 3 tbsp. chopped parsley
- 3 tbsp. breadcrumb coating
- Salt, freshly ground pepper

The real thing is made with beef. But why not try it with chicken or duck, seasoned with your favourite spices.

Cut the meat into cubes. Peel and chop the onions. Heat the oil in a casserole dish and brown the meat on all sides. Remove the meat, in its place fry half the onions (set the rest aside), then place the meat back in the casserole dish and pour in the red wine. Add the beef stock cube and top up with water. Simmer gently for 2 hours.

Wash the potatoes, cook them in water, with the skins on, for about 30 minutes until tender.

Filter 45 cl/1⅘ cups of stock through a sieve. Use a blender to grind the cooked meat – pulse to avoid reducing the meat to a puree. Peel and chop the shallots. Sauté with the remaining onions in 20g/1 heaped tbsp. butter until everything is soft. Add the ground meat and the remaining broth, season with salt and pepper, stir and simmer for 15 minutes. Preheat the oven to 300°F.

Heat the milk. Peel the potatoes and puree or mash until smooth. Add the warm milk to the mash, then 90 g/⅖ cup butter, then the cream. Season with salt and pepper. Grease a gratin dish with butter, spread out the layer of meat, sprinkle with chopped parsley, cover evenly with the potato puree, sprinkle the surface with breadcrumbs and small pieces of the remaining butter.

Bake for 20 minutes until the surface is golden.

CLASSIC
beef stew

- 3 turnips
- 3 large carrots
- 3 leeks
- 4 cabbage leaves
- 12 medium potatoes
- 1 onion
- 3 cloves
- 600 g/21 oz. short ribs of beef
- 600 g/21 oz. shoulder of beef (tied)
- 600 g/21 oz. chuck steak (tied)
- 1 sprig thyme
- 2 bay leaves
- Coarse salt
- 1 pinch black peppercorns

To serve
- Mustard
- Coarse salt

Wash and peel the vegetables. Cut the turnips in half and the carrots and leeks in three. Peel the onion and stud with cloves.

Put the meat in a cooking pot and cover with water. Add the onion studded with cloves, the thyme and bay leaf. Bring slowly to the boil and skim.

Add all vegetables except the potatoes. Cover and simmer gently for 3 hours. Season with a good pinch of coarse salt and cracked black pepper halfway through cooking. Add the potatoes 25 minutes before the end of cooking.

To serve, remove the meat from the broth and cut into slices, serve the vegetables and broth separately, all with coarse salt and strong mustard.

A dish in every French cook's repertoire. So essential, UNESCO made it part of the intangible cultural heritage of humanity.

CASSOULET

- 2 carrots
- 1 onion
- 1 clove garlic
- 1 cooking sausage
- 500 g/17 oz. shoulder of mutton
- 1 small knuckle of pork
- 250 g/9 oz. lightly cured streaky bacon
- 50 g/¼ cup duck or goose fat
- 1 tbsp. tomato puree
- 1 bouquet garni
- 50 g/2 oz. pork rind
- 500 g/17 oz. cooked white beans
- 5 tbsp. breadcrumbs
- Salt, pepper

Peel and chop the carrots into pieces. Peel the onion and garlic. Thinly slice the onion, finely chop the garlic.

Prick the cooking sausage with the tip of a fork. Cut the shoulder, knuckle of pork and streaky bacon into pieces. Heat the duck fat in a casserole dish and brown the pieces of meat. Add the sausage, carrots, onion, garlic, tomato puree and bouquet garni. Cover with water, season with salt and pepper, and simmer, covered, for 1 hour.

Preheat the oven to 400°F.

In a pot (preferably clay) or casserole dish, arrange the bacon rind, fat side down, alternately layer pieces of meat and beans. Drizzle with the cooking juices from the meat and sprinkle the top with breadcrumbs. Bake for 1 hour 30 minutes, basting regularly until a golden crust forms on the surface.

Where does the real cassoulet come from? That debate has been going on since the end of the 19th century. Our advice: don't worry about it! Just enjoy it with friends.

STUFFED
cabbage

- 1 small curly cabbage
- 150 g/2½ cups breadcrumbs
- 15 cl/⅝ cup milk
- 4 onions
- 3 tbsp. oil
- 300 g/10.5 oz. spare rib
  of pork
- 200 g/7 oz. smoked bacon
- 300 g/10.5 oz. sausage meat
- 3 tbsp. chopped parsley
- 1 large egg
- 10 cl/⅖ cup chicken stock
- 5 cl/⅕ cup white wine
- Salt, freshly ground pepper

Heat plenty of salted water. When it comes to the boil, immerse the cabbage, blanch for 10 minutes to soften the leaves. Drain the cabbage, dip in very cold water, place upside down in a colander to drain well. Select 12 fairly large leaves, remove any hard stalks.

Prepare the filling: soak the breadcrumbs in milk. Peel and finely chop the onions, gently fry in oil without browning. Finely chop the spare ribs and smoked bacon and combine with the sausage meat. Chop up the heart of the cabbage and add to the meat.

Squeeze any remaining water from the breadcrumbs then mix together with the chopped parsley, onions and egg (beaten). Season with salt and plenty of freshly ground pepper, stir well.

Make 12 stuffing balls, wrap each one in a cabbage leaf and a tight piece of cling film to ensure they hold their shape. Chill for 30 minutes.

Preheat the oven to around 410°F. Pour the chicken stock and white wine into a dish. Remove the cling film from the cabbage leaves and place them in the dish.

Bake for 35 minutes, basting regularly. Serve hot.

GARBURE

- 200 g/7 oz. white, dried or broad beans (preferably tarbais beans)
- 300 g/10.5 oz. salt pork
- 300 g/10.5 oz. cured ham
- 300 g/10.5 oz. ventrêche or streaky bacon
- 8 black peppercorns
- 1 stick celery
- 1 onion studded with 4 cloves
- 2 large cloves garlic
- 1 sprig thyme
- 1 bay leaf
- 3 carrots
- 2 turnips
- 4 confit duck legs
- 1 small cabbage cut into 4
- 400 g/14 oz. potatoes
- 4 slices crusty bread
- Salt, freshly ground pepper

Soak the dried beans for 12 hours in cold water. Rinse the salt pork. Remove the fat from the cured ham. Place the salt pork, cured ham and streaky bacon into a casserole dish or stewing pot. Add crushed peppercorns, celery, onion studded with cloves, peeled garlic, thyme and bay leaf. Pour in 4 litres of water and bring to the boil, skim off the foam several times, add the drained beans. Simmer for 4 hours.

Peel and wash the carrots and turnips. Cut into large pieces. Melt the fat from the duck legs in a pan over a low heat. Remove the meat, drain thoroughly and remove excess grease with paper towels. Fry the vegetables in 2 tbsp. duck fat for a few minutes, until they begin to brown. Drain and add them to the rest of the mixture. Halfway through cooking, add the duck legs.

Place the quartered cabbage in a saucepan and cover generously with cold water, slowly bring to the boil, blanch for 2 minutes then drain and strip off the leaves. Peel and wash the potatoes, cut into quarters. 30 minutes before the end of cooking, add them to the pot. 5 minutes before the end, add the cabbage leaves. When cooked, remove the meat and cut into pieces. Taste the soup and adjust the seasoning if necessary.

Arrange the slices of bread in the bottom of a soup tureen. Remove the onion, thyme and bay leaf and pour the soup into the tureen. Serve hot with the meat separate.

7 HOUR
ROAST LEG
of lamb

- 1 chicken stock cube
- 1 carrot
- 1 onion
- 3 tbsp. oil
- 1 leg of lamb (2 kg/4.4 lb)
- 200 g/7 oz. smoked bacon, cubed
- 1 bulb garlic
- 1 bouquet garni
- Salt, freshly ground pepper

Preheat the oven to 300°F.

Dissolve the stock cube in 25 cl/1 cup of hot water.
Peel and wash the vegetables, chop into large pieces.

Heat the oil in an ovenproof casserole dish and brown the lamb on all sides. Season with salt and pepper. Remove the lamb from the casserole dish and replace it with the vegetables, diced bacon and unpeeled garlic cloves. Fry for about 3 minutes while stirring and add the chicken stock and bouquet garni.

Return the lamb to the casserole dish, close the lid carefully to make sure it is airtight and bake for 7 hours, checking from time to time that there is still liquid in the casserole dish.

When the lamb is ready, remove it from the dish and keep it warm. Place the casserole dish on the heat, remove the grease from the cooking liquid with a slotted spoon, then deglaze the bottom of the pan using 10 cl/²⁄₅ cup of water. Reduce over a high heat for a few minutes. Spoon out the lamb and serve the sauce separately.

This dish speaks for itself.
Patience is the key word,
and it will be rewarded
when you taste
the tender meat.

MAGRETS
confits

- 3 duck breasts
- 4 tbsp. coarse salt
- 750 g/26 oz. duck
  or goose fat
- 1 sprig thyme
- 1 bay leaf
- Freshly ground black pepper
  or Espelette pepper

The night before, coat the duck breasts in coarse salt and place in an airtight container. Refrigerate for 12 hours.

The next day, gently wipe the duck with a clean cloth or paper towel. Quarter the skin with the tip of a sharp knife. Melt the duck fat in a casserole dish, arrange the duck breasts in the dish so that they do not overlap. Add the thyme and bay leaf, close the lid and leave to confit for 4 hours in the gently simmering fat. Baste occasionally.

Drain the duck breasts and brown in a pan. After cooking, drain again on a plate lined with paper towels. Season with pepper and serve with potatoes sautéed in duck fat.

If served cold as an aperitif, drain well and pat dry, then chill. Serve sliced and sprinkled with a little freshly ground pepper or Espelette pepper.

For an even more tender version, place the duck breasts in a large jar and cover with the cooking fat. Leave to cool, close the jar and refrigerate for 24 hours.

CHICKEN
WITH A CREAMY
mushroom sauce

- 60 g/¼ cup butter
- 1 drizzle oil
- 1 chicken, chopped into pieces
- 5 cl/⅕ cup dry white wine
- 500 g/17.5 oz. girolle
  mushrooms
- 20 cl/⅞ cup double cream
- 3 egg yolks
- Salt, freshly ground pepper

Heat 40 g/2 tbsp. butter with a little oil in a large frying pan or saucepan, brown the chicken pieces on all sides. Add the white wine, season with salt and pepper. Simmer over a low heat for 35 to 40 minutes. until the chicken is cooked. Preheat the oven to 120°F.

Prepare the mushrooms: cut off the earthy end and dry thoroughly with a brush until there are no traces of dirt left. Sweat for 5 minutes over a medium heat with the remaining butter. Keep warm.

Whip the cream with the egg yolks, season with salt and pepper.

When the chicken is cooked, remove from the pan, place in a dish, cover with foil and keep warm in the oven.

Deglaze the pan with a little water, reduce over a high heat then turn down the heat to a minimum. Wait a few minutes then add this mixture to the cream and mushrooms. Stir well and thicken over a low heat until the sauce is smooth. Taste and adjust seasoning if necessary. Pour the sauce over the chicken, mix and serve hot.

ROAST CHICKEN
WITH
sarladaise potatoes

For the roast chicken
- 1 chicken, around 1.3 kg/2.8 lb
- 3 tbsp. oil
- 15 g/1 tbsp. butter
- Salt, freshly ground pepper

For the sarladaise potatoes
- 800 g/28 oz. firm potatoes
- 60 g/¼ cup duck/goose fat
- 6 bunches parsley
- 2 cloves garlic
- Salt, freshly ground pepper

Crispy skin, tasty jus, and tender meat… not to mention how great it smells while it's cooking. Irresistible!

Preheat the oven to 410°F. Prick the chicken skin with the tip of a small knife. Place the chicken in a baking dish, drizzle with oil and sprinkle with knobs of butter. Season with salt. Bake for around 50 minutes (allow 20 minutes cooking time for 500g/17.5 oz. chicken), basting every 15 minutes. Turn halfway through cooking.

Peel the potatoes, wash and dry well, cut into thick slices. Heat 40 g/2 tbsp. of duck fat in a large frying pan and lightly brown the potatoes for around 15 minutes. Add the remaining duck fat, cover and simmer over a very low heat for another 15 minutes.

Remove the parsley leaves, chop with garlic. When the potatoes are soft, season with salt and pepper and sprinkle with the chopped parsley and garlic.

When the chicken is cooked, remove from the dish and keep warm. Place the baking dish on the stove and turn on the heat. Pour in 10 cl/²⁄₅ cup water, scraping the bottom of the pan to loosen the cooking juices. Thicken the sauce over a high heat for several minutes.

Cut the chicken and serve with the sauce in a separate dish, accompanied by the sarladaise potatoes.

TOASTED CHEESE
AND
ham sandwich

- 1 thick slice ham
- 25 g/2 tbsp. butter
- 2 slices sliced bread
- 1 slice processed cheese, designed for toasted sandwiches
- 25 g/¼ cup grated gruyère or emmental cheese
- 1 dash of oil
- Freshly ground pepper

Cut the slice of ham in 2. Lightly butter the bread on one side.

Layer 1 slice of bread with cheese and ham, season with pepper and sprinkle with grated gruyère. Top with the second slice of bread, gently pressing the croque monsieur together.

Lightly butter the top of the croque monsieur. Heat the remaining butter in a small pan with a drizzle of oil, place the croque-monsieur non-buttered side down and brown over a medium heat for around 3 minutes.

Turn with a spatula to brown the other side, again for 3 minutes. Press the top with a spatula to make the cheese melt faster.

Transfer to a plate, cut into triangles and serve with a well-seasoned salad.

First seen in 1910 in a Paris café, it has since been served in every cafe in France. Great at any time of day.

TARTIFLETTE

- 800 g/1.8 lb firm potatoes
- 200 g/7 oz. smoked bacon
- 2 onions
- 1 tbsp. oil
- 1 reblochon cheese
- 1 clove garlic
- 30 g/2 tbsp. double cream
- 15 cl/⅝ cup dry white wine
- Salt, pepper

Preheat the oven to 440°F.

Peel and rinse the potatoes, cook in salted water for 20 minutes after the water boils, until just done. Drain, leave to cool and cut into thick slices.

Cut the bacon into small pieces. Peel and chop the onions. Brown the bacon in a frying pan and drain off the fat. Add the oil and fry the onions.

Cut the Reblochon in two lengthways, then cut each half in 2 again.

Rub the bottom of a baking dish with the peeled garlic clove. Alternate layers of potatoes, onions and bacon.

Spread the cream evenly, season with pepper, then place the cheese slices on top with the crust up. Pour in the white wine and bake for 20-25 minutes.

STUFFED
tomatoes

- 6 medium tomatoes
- 1 large slice of bread
- 5 cl/⅕ cup milk
- 1 hard-boiled egg
- 1 clove garlic
- 2 shallots
- 5 bunches parsley
- 2 tbsp. oil
- 200 g/7 oz. finely minced veal
- 100 g/3.5 oz. finely minced ham
- 225 g/8 oz. sausage meat
- 15 cl/⅝ cup dry white wine
- 350 g/2 cups rice
- Salt, freshly ground pepper

Cut off the tops off the tomatoes, remove the flesh with a small spoon and set all aside. Season the inside of the tomatoes with salt and leave on a plate to disgorge during the preparation time.

Remove crust and soak the middle of the bread in milk. Peel and chop the hard-boiled egg. Peel the garlic and shallots. Rinse and dry the parsley. Finely chop all.

Heat the oil in a pan and fry the chopped ingredients for around 3 minutes. Add the veal, ham and sausage meat, cook for 10 minutes, regularly separating the meat with a fork to produce a fine stuffing mixture. Add the flesh of the tomatoes and simmer for another 5 minutes.

Remove from heat and stir in the chopped egg and bread (squeeze out excess milk), season with salt and pepper. Mix together well. Preheat the oven to 300°F.

Stuff the tomatoes, replace the tops. Arrange in a baking dish, well spaced. Pour in the white wine and cook for a good hour.

After 25 minutes, pour the rice into the bottom of the dish and add 1 glass of water. Serve hot.

ANDOUILLETTE
SAUSAGES
with mustard

- 2 shallots
- 1 tbsp. groundnut oil
- 4 andouillette sausages produced by the *Association amicale des amateurs d'andouillette authentique* (AAAAA)
- 1 glass dry white wine
- 3 tbsp. wholegrain mustard
- 20 cl/½ cup double cream
- Salt, pepper

Peel and finely chop the shallots.

Heat the oil in a casserole dish and brown the sausages on all sides. Add the shallots and stir for 2 minutes. Pour in the white wine and reduce the heat to a minimum. Season with salt and pepper. Cover the casserole dish and cook for 20 minutes, turning the sausages several times.

Remove the sausages and keep warm.

Put the mustard in the dish and stir well. Add the cream and mix for 3 minutes without letting it boil. Adjust seasoning if necessary. Add the sausages, cook on a low heat for 2 minutes and serve while hot.

France still seems to be the only nation producing sausages made from chitterlings. Production areas are found across the country, making this a dish to enjoy everywhere.

FROGS' LEGS
in cream sauce

- 1,5 kg/3.3 lb fresh frogs' legs
- 200 g/1⅔ cups flour
- 100 g/½ cup butter
- 3 finely chopped shallots
- 2 finely chopped cloves garlic
- 50 cl/2 cups cream
- 2 tsp. finely chopped chives
- Juice of ½ lemon
- Salt, pepper

Rinse the frogs' legs and dry on paper towels. Flour lightly. Melt the butter in a pan. Add the frogs' legs and brown over a medium heat.

Turn them two at a time to brown each side.

4 minutes into cooking, add the chopped shallots and garlic, leave to soften for a moment and then add half the cream, salt and pepper.

Stir gently and add the remaining cream. Keep warm.

To serve, add the chopped chives and lemon juice. Adjust seasoning if necessary.

Frogs made it onto French plates in the 16th century. So there is actually some truth behind the nickname 'frog eaters'!

POTATO GRATIN
with bacon

- 1.5 kg/3.3 lb firm potatoes
- 1 knob butter for the pan
- 6 rashers smoked bacon
- 30 cl/1¼ cups double cream
- 75 cl/3 cups milk
- 1 pinch freshly grated nutmeg
- Salt, freshly ground pepper

Peel, wash and dry the potatoes. Cut into slices 3 mm thick. Place into a bowl, season with salt and pepper, mix thoroughly so that everything is well seasoned.

Preheat the oven to 350°F.

Grease a large baking dish with butter and arrange the potatoes in rows, overlapping them. Place the bacon rashers at regular intervals between rows.

Whip the cream and milk together with a little salt, pepper and nutmeg.

Pour the mixture over the gratin and bake for around 45 to 50 minutes until the potatoes are soft and the surface of the gratin is lightly golden.

The success of this recipe lies in making sure the potatoes are cooked just right – slowly – to ensure they turn meltingly soft.

DUCHESS
potatoes

- 750 g/1.5 lb. floury potatoes
  (eg. Bintjes, Manon)
- 75 g/⅓ cup butter
- 1 pinch nutmeg
- 3 eggs + 1 yolk for egg wash
- Salt, freshly ground pepper

Peel and wash the potatoes, place in cold, salted water and cook for 20 minutes until done but still slightly firm.

Preheat the oven to 410°F.

Puree the potatoes with butter. Transfer to a saucepan and place over a low heat for 3 to 4 minutes to dry the mixture. Keep stirring. Season with salt, pepper and grated nutmeg.

Break the eggs, separate the whites from the yolks. Add the yolks to the mash. Beat the egg whites until stiff, then gently fold them into the mixture using a spatula.

Line a baking tray with baking paper.

Place the mash in a piping bag with a star tip (or a freezer bag with the corner cut off) and pipe small swirls of mash onto the tray.

Beat the egg yolk with 2 tsp. water and glaze the tops of the potato swirls.

Bake for 10-15 minutes until the duchess potatoes are golden brown. Serve as an accompaniment to meat or fish.

SOLE MEUNIÈRE

steamed potatoes

- 500 g/18 oz. small ratte potatoes
- 4 sole portions (ask the fishmonger to remove the dark skin and leave the white skin)
- 40 g/⅓ cup. flour
- 125 g/½ cup butter
- 2 cl/1 tbsp. oil
- Juice of 1 lemon
- 2 tbsp. chopped parsley
- Salt, freshly ground pepper

Peel and wash the potatoes, steam for about 15 minutes until tender. Keep warm.

Rinse and wipe the sole filets. Toss the filets in the flour and shake off any excess.

Set aside 40 g/2 tbsp. butter, cut the rest into pieces and place in a small saucepan. Heat gently. The butter will melt and turn golden. Stop cooking when you smell the butter browning.

Heat 2 large pans. When hot, melt the remaining butter with a drizzle of oil. Add the floured fish (white skin side first) and cook for 5 minutes over a medium heat, basting with the brown butter. Turn the fish and cook the other side for 5 minutes, again basting with butter.

Place on 4 warmed plates, sprinkle with lemon juice. Portion out the boiled potatoes. Strain the cooking juices through a small sieve, drizzle over the plate, season with salt and pepper and sprinkle with chopped parsley.

STUFFED
squid

- 9 squid, cleaned, with tentacles
- 125 g/2 cups breadcrumbs
  (grated from stale bread)
- 3 tomatoes
- 3 cloves garlic
- 4 shallots
- 130 g/4.5 oz. Bayonne ham
- 4 tbsp. olive oil
- 3 tbsp. chopped parsley
- 2 pinches Espelette pepper
- 25 cl/1 cup dry white wine
- 1 bay leaf

Rinse the squid thoroughly and drain well. Soak the bread crumbs in a little warm water. Boil the tomatoes, peel, remove the seeds and cut into small cubes.

Prepare the stuffing: chop the meat and tentacles of one squid. Peel the garlic and shallots, remove the fat from the Bayonne ham. Chop all of these finely.

Heat 2 tbsp. oil in a pan and fry the chopped squid for 2 to 3 minutes. Then add the garlic, shallots, ham and 2 tbsp. chopped parsley. Sauté together for about 5 minutes, stirring well. When the stuffing is cooked, thoroughly drain the breadcrumbs in a fine sieve and add to the stuffing. Season with 1 pinch of Espelette pepper.

Fill the squid with the stuffing, taking care not to puncture the skin. Close the opening with a toothpick. Heat the remaining oil in a casserole dish and fry the squid. Add the diced tomatoes, white wine and bay leaf and cook over a very low heat for 25 minutes.

Serve hot, sprinkled with Espelette pepper and the remaining chopped parsley.

MOULES
marinière

- 1 onion
- 4 shallots
- 2 cloves garlic
- 1 bunch parsley
- 1 sprig thyme
- 1 bay leaf
- 1 stick celery
- 30 g/2 tbsp. butter
- 4 litres/5.5 lb mussels, scrubbed and washed
- 20 cl/⅞ cup dry white wine
- Salt, freshly ground pepper

Peel and chop the onion, shallots and garlic cloves.

Remove the parsley leaves, tie the stalks together with the thyme and bay leaf to make a bouquet garni. Finely chop the parsley leaves.

Wash the celery and cut into small pieces.

Melt the butter in a pot and sweat the onion, garlic, shallots, celery and half the parsley. Add the bouquet garni.

Put the mussels in the pot, stir for a few minutes then add the white wine, salt and pepper. Raise the temperature and stir over a high heat until the mussels are wide open.

Sprinkle with the remaining parsley and serve with fries.

Simple, tasty, and cheap. And as an added bonus, there's no need for a knife and fork – eating with your fingers is recommended.

COD
brandade

- 500 g/1 lb cod
- 500 g/1 lb potatoes
- 50 g/¼ cup butter
- 70 cl/3 cups milk
- 8 sprigs parsley
- 1 clove garlic
- Breadcrumbs
- Salt, pepper

The night before, leave the cod to desalinate in cold water, changing the water several times.

On the day of cooking, bring 50 cl/2 cups milk to a boil and poach the cod for 5 minutes. Drain and set aside the cooking milk.

Crumble the cod with a fork, removing the skin and any bones.

Peel the potatoes and cut into large cubes. Cook in a pan of boiling salted water for 25 minutes. Drain and mash in a bowl with a potato masher. Add the butter and remaining milk and stir until the mixture is nice and smooth.

Wash and finely chop the parsley. Peel and chop the garlic. Preheat the oven to 350°F.

Stir the cod, parsley and garlic into the puree, add 20 cl/⅞ cup of the reserved cooking milk and stir. Season with pepper and some salt if necessary (do not over salt as the cod will stay salty).

Place the mixture in a gratin dish, sprinkle with breadcrumbs and bake for 20 minutes. Serve hot.

PIKE QUENELLES
with Nantua sauce

For the quenelles
- 25 cl/1 cup milk
- 80 g/1/3 cup butter+butter for the dish
- 125 g/ ½ cup flour
- 5 eggs
- 250 g/9 oz. pike flesh
- 3 tbsp. thick double cream
- Salt, pepper

For the Nantua sauce
- 30 g/2 tbsp. butter
- 30 g/¼ cup flour
- 50 cl/2 cups milk
- 50 g/3 tbsp double cream
- 1 tbsp. crayfish butter

If you're ever passing through Lyon, get out of your traffic jam and order this dish, the jewel in the crown of Lyon's cuisine.

Boil the milk and butter in a saucepan, season with salt and pepper. Sprinkle in the flour and whisk. When the mixture begins to stiffen, reduce the heat and work it with a spatula. Remove pan from heat and add 3 eggs. Mix and leave to cool.

Place the pike flesh in a blender, season with salt and pepper. Add this puree to the previous preparation and mix. Stir in the remaining eggs. Add the cream and stir until the mixture appears even. Leave this paste to stand in the refrigerator for around 2 hours.

Shape the quenelles by rolling them between moistened palms.

Prepare the Nantua sauce: melt the butter over a low heat. Add the flour, stir until the mixture is frothy. Add the cold milk in one go, season with salt and pepper. Stir until thick and cook on a low heat for around 10 minutes. Mix in the double cream and crayfish butter. Stir well. Keep warm.

Heat a large pan of salted water. When it begins to simmer, submerge the quenelles and allow 15 minutes to poach. When cooked, they float to the surface. Preheat the oven to 350°F.

Drain on a cloth. Butter a gratin dish and pour in half the Nantua sauce. Place the quenelles on top, then cover with the remaining sauce. Bake for around 10 minutes. Serve the quenelles nice and hot.

Desserts

BRIOCHE

- 110 g/½ cup butter + 1 knob for the pan
- 10 g/1 level tbsp. fresh yeast
- 5 cl/⅕ cup warm milk
- 250 g/2 cups flour
- 1 tsp. salt
- 30 g/2 tbsp. sugar
- 2 medium eggs+1 yolk

Remove the butter from the fridge, cut into small pieces and leave at room temperature.

Dissolve the yeast in the warm milk. Pour the flour into a deep bowl (or better still, a dough mixer), make a well in the middle and add the salt, sugar, dissolved yeast and eggs. Knead the mixture for about ten minutes until the dough is smooth and not sticky (add a little flour if necessary). Add butter and knead quickly to mix it in without melting. Make the dough into a ball and place in a bowl, cover the bowl with cling film to prevent a crust forming and leave to stand for 1 hour in a warm place.

Grease a cake tin or loaf tin. When the dough has doubled in size, knead quickly again and place into the tin. Let the dough rise, covered with cling film, until it has again doubled in size.

Preheat the oven to 350°F. Beat the egg yolk with 2 tsp. water and glaze the top of the brioche. Bake for around 35 minutes until golden.

Turn out the brioche when cooled, but still warm.

SWEET
fritters

- 8 g/1 heaped tsp. yeast
- 2 tbsp. milk at room temperature
- 250 g/2 cups flour+1 tbsp.
- 40 g/2 level tbsp. caster sugar
- 1 pinch salt
- 2 eggs
- 1 tbsp. orange blossom
- 1 tsp. lemon zest
- 60 g/¼ cup softened butter
- Frying oil
- 3 tbsp. icing sugar

Crumble the yeast into the milk and leave to stand for 10 minutes.

Mix the flour, sugar, and salt in a large bowl, add the beaten eggs, yeast, orange blossom and lemon zest. Knead, then add the butter cut into pieces. Knead again for 15 minutes, until the dough is nice and soft. Make the dough into a ball and place it into a deep bowl. Cover the bowl with cling film and leave to stand for 30 minutes at room temperature.

Flour the work surface and rolling pin. Roll out the pastry to a thickness of 2 cm. Using a serrated pastry wheel, cut rectangles of 7x4 cm, make an indentation in the middle. Place the rectangles on a sheet of baking paper and leave to rise for another 30 minutes, again covered with cling film.

To ensure the fritters hold their shape, place them in the refrigerator for 15 minutes to firm the dough before frying.

Prepare a pan of hot oil and fry the fritters until golden, turning once halfway through cooking.

Drain on paper towels. Serve the fritters sprinkled with icing sugar.

These fritters, originally from Lyon, were traditionally made and eaten on feast days, especially for Mardi Gras.

MACARONS

For coffee buttercream
- 150 g/⅔ cup butter
  at room temperature
- 4 egg yolks
- 6 cl/⅕ cup of water
- 150 g/⅔ cup caster sugar
- A few drops of coffee extract

For chocolate buttercream
- 150 g/⅔ cup butter
  at room temperature
- 4 egg yolks
- 150 g/⅔ cup caster sugar
- 75 g/2.5 oz. dark chocolate
  (70% cocoa)

For the shells
- 75 g/⅔ cup icing sugar
- 75 g/2.5 oz. powdered
  almonds
- 2 medium egg whites
- Powdered food colouring,
  coffee and chocolate (optional)
- 75 g/⅓ cup caster sugar

Prepare the coffee buttercream: work the butter with a fork until it has a creamy consistency. Beat the egg yolks in a bowl. Pour the sugar and water into a pan, heat to 233°F to produce a syrup.

Drizzle the hot syrup over the egg yolks while whisking. Keep whisking until the mixture has completely cooled and tripled in size. Add the creamed butter and the coffee extract. Mix well until smooth. Leave the mixture to cool and refrigerate.Repeat the process for the chocolate buttercream, substituting the coffee extract with chocolate, simply melted in a bain marie without overheating.

Prepare the macaron shells: mix together the icing sugar and almond powder. Add an egg white, and a drop of food colouring if desired, and leave to rest. Beat the second egg white until stiff. Pour the caster sugar into a saucepan, add a few drops of water. Heat to 240°F. Then drizzle the syrup over the egg white, beating until the mixture forms peaks. Gently fold the egg white into the icing sugar/almond powder mixture.

Pour the mixture into a pastry bag. Line 2 baking trays with baking paper and pipe out the macarons in small circles 4 cm in diameter, spacing well. Preheat the oven to 300°F. Let your macarons dry for 20 minutes, then bake for 12 minutes. Open the oven door twice during cooking to let the moisture escape. Remove the macarons from the baking tray and assemble with either coffee or chocolate buttercream.

KOUGLOF

- 1 tbsp. kirsch
- 5 cl/⅕ cup of water
- 70 g/2.5 oz. raisins
- 12 g/1 tbsp. fresh yeast
- 50 cl/2 cups warm milk
- 300 g/2 ½ cups flour
- 40 g/2 tbsp. sugar
- ½ tsp. salt
- 1 egg
- 100 g/½ cup butter at room temperature + 1 knob for the pan
- 12 whole almonds
- 1 tbsp. icing sugar

Pour the kirsch into a bowl, add the raisins and the water. Cover the bowl and let the raisins rehydrate for 30 minutes.

Prepare a leaven by crumbling the yeast into the milk, add one third of the flour, stir, cover the bowl and leave to rise for 45 minutes in a warm place.

Mix the remaining flour with the sugar, salt and egg (beaten). Add the yeast. Knead for 10 minutes then add the butter cut into pieces. Knead again until the dough is nice and smooth.

Drain the raisins well and add them to the dough. Place in a bowl, cover with cling film. Leave the dough to rise for at least 1 hour in a warm place.

Grease and flour a kouglof or brioche tin. Place one almond in the bottom of each groove. Roll the dough into a ball and place it in the tin. Leave to rise for 1 hour until doubled in volume. Preheat the oven to around 320°F, then cook the mixture for 40 to 45 minutes.

Leave to cool for around ten minutes before placing a plate over the kouglof to turn it out of the tin. Sprinkle with icing sugar.

Served with a glass of wine from its native Alsace region, this raisin brioche is sure to impress. At its best on the second day, when it is a little stale.

MADELEINES

- 150 g/⅔ cup lightly salted butter+15 g/1 tbsp. for the tins
- 5 eggs
- 150 g/⅔ cup caster sugar
- 150 g/1¼ cups flour
- 1 tbsp. orange blossom water

Preheat the oven to 460°F.

Gently melt the butter over a low heat.

Break the eggs and separate the whites from the yolks. Beat the egg whites until stiff.

Beat the yolks with sugar until pale, add the melted butter, sprinkle in the flour and add the orange blossom water. Whisk well to give a light mixture and gently fold in the egg whites, lifting with a spatula. Let the dough rest for at least 12 hours (preferably 24 hours).

Grease 2 twelve-cup madeleine tins and fill with the mixture. Bake at 460°F for 5 minutes then turn down the oven to 410°F and cook for another 10 minutes.

Turn out the madeleines while hot and leave to cool on a rack.

A sweet treat originally from Commercy in Lorraine, the madeleine owes its popularity to Marcel Proust.

CRÈME
caramel

- 75 g/⅓ cup sugar
- 1 egg
- 10 cl/⅖ cup milk
- 5 cl/⅕ cup single cream
- ½ tsp. natural vanilla extract

Pour 30 g/2 tbsp. sugar into a small saucepan, add 1 tsp. water. Gently rotate the pan so that the sugar is completely soaked. Cook over a medium heat until the mixture forms an amber coloured caramel. Immediately place the caramel into the bottom of a ramekin.

Whisk the egg with the remaining sugar until the mixture turns white.

Pour the milk and cream into a saucepan, add the vanilla extract. Stir and bring to the boil. Pour the boiling mixture over the beaten egg, whisking until the mixture is smooth. Filter through a fine sieve and pour into the ramekin, on top of the caramel.

Preheat the oven to 350°F. Place the ramekin in a baking dish. Add boiling water up to two thirds of the height of the ramekin. Bake for about 25 minutes until the custard is set.

Remove the ramekin from the oven, let it cool in the bain marie. Chill for at least 1 hour.

Gently slide a knife around the cream and turn out upside-down onto a plate.

EGG
custard tart

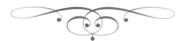

- 80 cl/3⅓ cups milk
- 20 cl/⅞ cup single cream
- 5 eggs
- 90 g/½ cup caster sugar
- 1 tbsp. vanilla extract
- 60 g/½ cup cornflour

For the shortcrust pastry
- 250 g/2 cups flour
- 125 g/½ cup softened butter
  +1 knob for the pan
- 5 g/1 tsp. salt
- 5 cl/⅕ cup water

Prepare the pastry: pour the flour into a deep bowl and make a well. In the centre, add the softened butter cut into pieces and the salt. Rub the mixture using your fingertips and then add water. Knead quickly until the dough is soft and smooth. Make the dough into a ball, wrap in cling film and leave in the refrigerator for 2 hours.

Remove the pastry from the fridge and leave to soften for 15 minutes. Preheat the oven to 350°F.

Roll out the pastry until 0.5 cm thick. Grease a tin with butter and lay out the pastry. Prick the bottom with a fork a few times, cover with a sheet of baking paper and hold in place with dried pulses or baking beads. Bake for 10 minutes then remove the weights and continue cooking for 5 minutes.

Heat the milk and cream until the mixture just begins to simmer. Beat the eggs with the sugar and vanilla extract until the mixture turns white. Stir in the cornflour and add the boiling milk and cream while whisking. Pour the mixture into a saucepan and gently bring to the boil while still whisking. When the mixture begins to simmer, remove from the heat and pour into the pastry case. Bake for 30 minutes, the flan is cooked when the dough is brown and the cream is set. Leave to cool before refrigerating overnight.

CHOCOLATE
charlotte

- 4 eggs
- 50 g/½ cup icing sugar
- 50 g/¼ cup lightly salted butter+1 knob for the pan
- 125 g/4 oz. dark chocolate (70% cocoa)
- 15 cl espresso
- 3 tbsp. Grand Marnier® or cognac
- 24 ladyfinger biscuits
- Custard to serve

For the topping
- 15 cl whipping cream
- 150 g/5 oz. chocolate

Break the eggs, separate the white from the yolk. Beat the egg whites until stiff. When they start to firm up, gradually add the icing sugar and keep whisking. Cut the butter and chocolate into pieces. Melt together in a simmering bain marie until the mixture is smooth and creamy. Whisk the egg yolks until frothy, add them to the melted chocolate. Then add ⅓ of the beaten egg whites, stirring vigorously, and add the rest gradually, folding gently with a spatula. Mix the coffee and alcohol of your choice in a deep dish.

Dip half the ladyfinger biscuits quickly into this mixture, then place them on the edges and bottom of the tin. Spread half the chocolate mousse over the first layer of biscuits. Dip more biscuits in the coffee and use them to make another layer. Add the remaining mousse and finish with a layer of ladyfingers soaked in coffee. Tap the tin on the worktop to pack down the contents, then place a plate on top. Refrigerate for 12 hours.

Prepare the topping: heat the whipping cream, cut up the chocolate and cover with the hot cream, stirring to produce a smooth creamy mixture.

Turn out the charlotte, coat it with chocolate and serve with custard.

CHOCOLATE
cake

- 70 g/⅗ cup flour
- 1 tsp. baking powder
- 1 pinch salt
- 250 g/9 oz. good quality dark chocolate (min. 70% cocoa)
- 150 g/⅔ cup butter + 1 knob for the tin
- 5 eggs
- 170 g/⅔ cup caster sugar
- 1 tsp. vanilla extract

Preheat the oven to 350°F.

Mix the flour, baking powder and salt.

Chop the chocolate roughly and melt in a bain marie together with the butter cut into small pieces. Smooth out the mixture evenly with a spatula. Transfer to a large bowl. Leave to cool for a few minutes then add the eggs one by one, mixing well each time. Sprinkle in the flour, stir, then add the icing sugar and vanilla extract.

Grease a cake tin with butter and distribute the mixture evenly. Bake for 20 to 25 minutes. Be careful not to overcook the cake to keep it soft: check that it's done by sliding in the blade of a knife, it should come out without any sticky traces of mixture but still slightly moist.

Once out of the oven, let the cake rest before turning it out, still warm, onto a cooling rack.

POUND CAKE
MADE WITH
salted butter

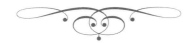

- 160 g/1⅓ cups flour
- 2 tsp. baking powder
- 160 g/⅔ cup softened lightly
  salted butter+1 knob for
  the pan
- 160 g/¾ cup sugar
- 3 medium eggs

Preheat the oven to 300°F.

Mix the flour and baking powder.

Grease a cake tin with butter.

Work the butter with a fork until it takes on the consistency of a cream, then add the sugar. Mix well until smooth.

Add the eggs one by one, mixing every time. Stir in the flour gradually. When the mixture is smooth, pour it into the cake tin.

Bake for 40 to 45 minutes. Check that the cake is done by inserting the blade of a knife, it should come out clean, without any traces of mixture.

TARTE
Tatin

- 100 g/1.2 cup butter + 1 knob
  for the pan
- 2 kg/4.4 lb apples
- 200 g/1 cup caster sugar
- 1 egg for egg wash

For shortcrust pastry
- 150 g/1 ¼ cups flour
- 75 g/⅓ cup butter
- 1 pinch salt
- 2.5 cl/1.5 tbsp. water

Prepare the shortcrust pastry: place the flour into a large bowl, make a well for the butter (cut into pieces) and salt. Work the mixture with the fingertips then add water. Knead quickly to form a smooth dough, make a ball and wrap it in cling film. Leave to rest for 2 hours in the refrigerator. Preheat the oven to 410°F.

Melt the butter in a small saucepan.

Peel the apples and cut into thick wedges. Grease a tin (unless using a non-stick tin), sprinkle the bottom with half the sugar and arrange the apple wedges. Sprinkle evenly with the remaining sugar and baste with melted butter. Cook over a medium heat until a golden caramel appears, then turn off the heat.

Remove the dough from the refrigerator 15 minutes before rolling it out to a thickness of 5 mm, then cut a circle the size of your tin. Place the circle over the apples. Using the handle of a teaspoon, evenly press the edges of the pastry closed around the apples. Beat the egg and glaze the top of the dough.

Bake at 410°F for 25 minutes. Leave to stand for a few minutes, then turn out the tarte.

Serve with double cream, whipped cream or vanilla ice cream.

We shall always be grateful to the Tatin sisters, who one day ruined a classic apple tart by forgetting to put the pastry in the bottom of the tin! Sometimes it doesn't take much to come up with a great recipe!

SPICE
bread

- 125 g/½ cup butter+1 knob for the pan
- 100 g/⅓ cup honey
- 15 cl/⅝ cup milk
- 200 g/1⅔ cups flour
- 1 pinch salt
- 2 tsp. baking powder
- 50 g/¼ cup brown sugar
- 8 g/1 tsp. pain d'épice spice mix (a blend of aniseed, cloves, nutmeg, cinnamon)
- 1 egg

Preheat the oven to 350°F.

Grease a cake tin with butter.

Heat the honey, milk and butter, stir.

Mix the flour, salt, baking powder, brown sugar and spices in a bowl. Gradually add the honey/milk/butter mixture, whisking gently. Work the mixture well until smooth and even. Add the egg, beaten.

Pour the mixture into the tin and bake for 40–45 minutes.

Turn out the spice bread and leave to cool on a rack.

Evokes winter, evenings by the fireside and Christmas parties. Makes a delicious snack with tea or, if you really want to indulge, a hot chocolate.

FRENCH TOAST
WITH HOMEMADE
caramel spread

- 1 tin condensed milk
- 1 egg
- 15 cl/⅝ cup milk
- 1 tsp. sugar
- 15 g/1 tbsp. butter
- 1 dash of oil
- 2 thick slices stale bread
- 1 sachet vanilla sugar

Prepare the caramel spread: place the tin of condensed milk in a saucepan and cover well with water. Bring to the boil and cook for 2 hours, making sure that the tin is always submerged. After cooking, remove the tin from the pan and leave to cool completely before opening (danger of burns). Then open the tin, pour the contents into a large bowl and work with a fork to make a smooth cream. Put the cream in a glass jar.

Whisk the egg with the milk and sugar.

Heat the butter and oil in a frying pan. Dip the bread in milk on both sides until just moistened. Brown the slices of bread in the butter, turning halfway through cooking.

Sprinkle with vanilla sugar and eat hot or warm with your homemade caramel spread.

Keep the caramel spread refrigerated in a sealed jar and consume within 5 days.

This dessert, once seen as food for the poor, since it used up stale bread that would otherwise be thrown away, has been rediscovered and is now served at top restaurants.

Serves **6** / Preparation: **10** min / Cooking: **1** h **5**

CARAMEL rice pudding

- 250 g/1¼ cups caster sugar
- 90 cl/3¾ cups milk
- 1 large vanilla pod
- 180 g/1 cup pudding rice

Preheat the oven to 350°F.

Prepare the caramel: put 200 g/1 cup sugar in a saucepan, add 7 cl/⅓ cup water and place over a medium heat, stirring gently from time to time until the caramel turns a nice amber colour. Transfer to a heavy-bottomed pan or cooking pot.

Put the milk and remaining sugar in a saucepan. Open the vanilla pod and extract the seeds, add the seeds and pod to the contents of the pan. Bring to the boil, then sprinkle in the rice. Mix and bring back to the boil, then cook over a low heat for 10 minutes, stirring frequently.

Remove the vanilla pod and transfer the rice pudding to the pan, on top of the caramel. Bake for 50 minutes.

During cooking, stir 2 or 3 times to incorporate the skin that forms on the surface of the mixture.

Serve warm or cold.

CRÊPES
Suzette

- 1 orange (untreated)
- 20 cl/⅞ cup of water
- 30 cl/1¼ cup milk
- 2 eggs
- 30 g/2 tbsp. sugar
- 1 generous pinch salt
- 200 g/1⅔ cups flour
- 50 g/¼ cup cooled melted butter
- 1 tbsp. sunflower oil

For the sauce
- 90 g/⅖ cup butter
- 90 g/½ cup sugar
- The juice of 3 oranges
- 20 cl/⅞ cup Grand Marnier®

Zest the orange and squeeze. Mix the milk with the water. Beat the eggs together with the salt and sugar. Stir in one third of the milk and water mixture. Add the flour in batches, whisking vigorously to avoid lumps. Pour in the melted butter, stir, then add the remaining milk and water mixture followed by the orange juice and zest. Cover with a cloth and leave to stand for 1 hour at room temperature.

Grease the pan with a piece of kitchen towel soaked in oil, heat until the pan is nice and hot. Beat the batter and pour one ladleful into the pan. After 1 minute, flip the pancake and cook the other side for around 30 seconds. Transfer to a plate, fold the crepe into a triangle. Repeat with the remaining batter, greasing the pan between each pancake.

Melt the butter with the sugar in a saucepan, add the orange juice, let the mixture reduce for 2 to 3 minutes. Pour a little sauce into a frying pan, enough to generously cover the bottom, place 4 crepes into the pan and let them warm up, on a medium heat, basting them with the sauce. Pour in 5 cl/⅕ cup Grand Marnier®, and flambé. When the flame goes out, transfer the pancakes to a warm plate, top them with the remaining sauce from the pan, and cover to keep them nice and warm. Repeat with the remaining crepes and sauce. Serve hot.

INDEX